CW00660324

Public Talk Series: 4

DISCOVERING LOVE

Swami Dayananda Saraswati
Arsha Vidya

Arsha Vidya
Research and Publication Trust
Chennai

Published by :
Arsha Vidya Research
and Publication Trust
4 'Sri Nidhi' Apts, III Floor
Sir Desika Road, Mylapore
Chennai 600 004, India
Tel   : 044 24997023
Telefax : 044 24997131
Email   : avrandpt@gmail.com
Website : www.avrpt.com

ISBN: 978 - 93 - 80049 - 02 - 1

First Edition : June   2006 Copies : 2000
1st Reprint   : May   2009 Copies : 2000
2nd Reprint   : February 2011 Copies : 1000
3rd Reprint   : July   2013 Copies : 1000
4th Reprint   : January   2017 Copies : 1000

Design & layout :
Graaphic Design

Printed by :
Sudarsan Graphics
27, Neelakanta Mehta Street
T. Nagar, Chennai – 600 017
Email: print@sudarsan.com

CONTENTS

PREFACE

I am very happy to see in print the series of talks I gave in Chennai under different titles for meaningful 'Living'. I enjoyed my reading these manuscripts inasmuch as the material therein was an outcome of my open thinking. In fact in some places I was amused as well as surprised. Anyone who reads this book, I am sure, will find it refreshingly useful. I congratulate the dedicated people at the Arsha Vidya Research and Publication Trust, for this thoughtful publication.

Swami Dayananda Saraswati

Rishikesh
27 May 2006

KEY TO TRANSLITERATION AND PRONUNCIATION OF
SANSKRIT LETTERS

Sanskrit is a highly phonetic language and hence accuracy in articulation of the letters is important. For those unfamiliar with the *Devanägari* script, the international transliteration is a guide to the proper pronunciation of Sanskrit letters.

अ	a	(b*u*t)	ट	öa	(*t*rue)*3
आ	ä	(f*a*ther)	ठ	öha	(an*t*hill)*3
इ	i	(*i*t)	ड	òa	(*d*rum)*3
ई	é	(b*ea*t)	ढ	òha	(go*dh*ead)*3
उ	u	(f*u*ll)	ण	ëa	(u*n*der)*3
ऊ	ü	(p*oo*l)	त	ta	(pa*th*)*4
ऋ	å	(*r*hythm)	थ	tha	(*th*under)*4
ॠ	è	(ma*ri*ne)	द	da	(*th*at)*4
ऌ	ÿ	(reve*lr*y)	ध	dha	(breat*he*)*4
ए	e	(pl*ay*)	न	na	(*n*ut)*4
ऐ	ai	(*ai*sle)	प	pa	(*p*ut) 5
ओ	o	(g*o*)	फ	pha	(loo*ph*ole)*5
औ	au	(lo*u*d)	ब	ba	(*b*in) 5
क	ka	(see*k*) 1	भ	bha	(a*bh*or)*5
ख	kha	(bloc*kh*ead)*1	म	ma	(*m*uch) 5
ग	ga	(*g*et) 1	य	ya	(lo*y*al)
घ	gha	(lo*g h*ut)*1	र	ra	(*r*ed)
ङ	ìa	(si*ng*) 1	ल	la	(*l*uck)
च	ca	(*ch*unk) 2	व	va	(*v*ase)
छ	cha	(cat*ch h*im)*2	श	ça	(*s*ure)
ज	ja	(*j*ump) 2	ष	ña	(*sh*un)
झ	jha	(he*dg*ehog)*2	स	sa	(*s*o)
ञ	ïa	(bu*n*ch) 2	ह	ha	(*h*um)

•	à	*anusvära*	(nasalisation of preceding vowel)
:	ù	*visarga*	(aspiration of preceding vowel)
*			No exact English equivalents for these letters

1.	Guttural	–	Pronounced from throat
2.	Palatal	–	Pronounced from palate
3.	Lingual	–	Pronounced from cerebrum
4.	Dental	–	Pronounced from teeth
5.	Labial	–	Pronounced from lips

The 5th letter of each of the above class – called nasals – are also pronounced nasally.

vii

Talk 1

Introduction

Love is a very ancient topic. The Vedic sages, playwrights, musicians and poets have glorified the word love, and its meaning. Love is not an emotion that is on par with the others. It is not that there are many emotions of which one is love, which is precisely why you need to discover love. Love is the only emotion which in certain forms is called compassion, empathy and sympathy. It is the same love that accommodates another person. It is love which also provides you the space to understand another person. It is love that really turns into hatred, turns into your dislike, anger and so on. Love appears to stifle, strangulate, and is more painful than ennobling. Poets and artists often speak or express love as pain and anguish, the anguish of unrequited love, lost love, missing love, and love that cannot be found. Love appears to defy all reason and logic · inasmuch as it induces people to even destroy themselves and others. It is one emotion which has these various positive and negative expressions. Love is not something to be swallowed, like you have swallowed many things. Love has to be discovered.

You know very well, emotions have neither nationality, provenance, culture, history, gender nor age. Such factors do not inhibit the nature of a given emotion in any way. For instance if we take anger, be it royal or plebeian, be it in a child or in an adult, its nature and vision do not differ; it is anger. Emotions such as anger, hatred, compassion, sympathy and love, in their simple forms, have always been there. A cat is always affectionate and so is a dog. They express their emotions, express how much they missed you and so on. If animals can express emotions, how much more can a human being? A human being is the most self-conscious of life forms. Naturally, in a human heart emotions are very well pronounced.

When you encounter the world, you do not remain a mute witness; you actively respond to persons, objects and situations. The response is not always dispassionate or totally objective, like a computer. The emotional person that you are, always inhibits the response. Emotions, therefore, form the basic theme of an individual's biography. They drive you to accomplish, no doubt, but they also subject you to a sense of failure and depression. There are times when you just want to quit. In short, emotions drive you crazy. To have a complete mastery over your emotions always remains a dream. Emotions make the person, much more than even cognition does. In fact, they sweep aside the cognitive person and take over. Emotions are what you are, what you have. The emotional person is the core person and it is this core person who feels that he or she is useless. It is also the very same person who complicates his or her life as well as the life of others.

DURYODHANA - A CASE STUDY OF A CHILD
DEPRIVED OF LOVE

If you look into the *Mahābhārata*, you will find that the individuals' behaviour, the causes of war were all emotional.

Duryodhana, for instance, did not have a father who could see him, who could applaud and make him feel good about him. His father was blind.

A child is born helpless, totally helpless, and so it is endowed with this great capacity to trust totally. Total trust implies that the trusted person, in the eyes of the child, is infallible, almighty. Infallible means the person cannot fail and cannot fall ill. It is this infallibility that a child sees in the person it trusts. It cannot totally trust a person who has limitations, who fails. The child starts its life with absolute helplessness. It cannot survive without help. It needs to be held by loving hands and brought up for years. Therefore, the child cannot afford to distrust, if it has to survive. This total helplessness is compensated properly in the setup that we call the *jagat*, the world.

The human child is self-conscious. Self-consciousness naturally results in self-judgement. From the child's standpoint, everyone around is bigger, more capable and therefore, better. With its limited knowledge, it judges itself to be insignificant and useless. This is how the human child starts his or her life, that he or she is useless. The child may be a prince or an average citizen, but this is the starting point. However, this sense of inadequacy is neutralised to a large extent by the parents, who are Gods for the child. Their approval, their welcoming the child as a blessing, as a gift, enables the child to handle this feeling of being useless.

Further, the parents, as creators, participate in and share the joy of creation. Their joy is expressed in their approval, their care and concern, although the expression is often inhibited by their anxieties and ambitions for the future of the child. But their approval and care are not actualised in a manner that the child can understand. In their anxiety for the child's future, the parents are often so busy that they have little or no time for the child. It is not a surprise, then, if the child grows into a Duryodhana. The child needs the express approval of its parents. The father has to look into the child's eyes and make it feel that it has brought joy to the home; that it has enriched their life. It is this approval, to a large extent, offsets the child's sense of inadequacy. If a child jumps from a ledge or a table, no matter how low, it has a sense of achievement. It looks to its parents for approval. In their approval and applause the child's sense of inadequacy decreases and it visibly flowers. As a result, perhaps, society gains a sane member. We contribute to the increasing neurosis in society by neglecting these basic principles.

Unlike the professional world, there is no specific training to be a parent. You learn on the job, a time tested trial and error method. In a joint-family system, you observe and learn by the law of osmosis as it were. You watch many family members, their interactions and so on, and replicate these in your life. Unfortunately, contemporary society has lost the traditional family support system. What was valid in a joint family is no longer valid in a nuclear family situation. There are no aunts or grandparents either for the child or for the parents to seek help, advice or comfort. The young parents are forced to turn on themselves to find solutions to the problems they face. By trial and error, they figure out how to bring up an emotionally healthy, confident child; a child that has a sense of being wanted, of contributing to the joy of the parents and of the home. Parents must pay attention to this aspect of a child's upbringing if they want their child to be self-accepting, self-confident.

Duryodhana was deprived of such parental care and approval. Even if his father was not available, his mother could have stepped in. Unfortunately for him, she did not. A misguided sense of loyalty made her blindfold herself. Some people praise her. Perhaps there was some good in it but as a result, poor Duryodhana was denied a mother's appreciation. She was a good wife; it is true. In fact, her husband approved, "I cannot see and now you too cannot. I am very happy." What kind of man was he? He should have said, "Be my eyes." She should have been his eyes and ears. Blindfolding herself was a mistake, a mistake born of emotions. The entire *Mahābhārata* is a tragedy because it is a series of mistakes that people committed out of emotions. Karṇa is a case in point.

I have looked into the original *Mahābhārata* and found that Karṇa is a character to study. He was an abandoned child even though he was a born prince with the blessings of lord Sun. Circumstances were such that he was brought up as a *sūta-putra*, son of charioteer. However, Karṇa never felt at ease with his foster family. He knew that there was something different; he just did not belong. He always felt different. He felt that he was better than any of the *kṣatriyas* around. He could not bear to be called a *sūta-putra*; his very being rebelled against it. When others around him addressed him or referred to him as *sūta-putra*, he felt it was unjust and seethed with suppressed anger. So he desperately wanted to make a mark to achieve and be better than anybody, so that he could overcome this feeling. He said in one place, 'I give because I want people to tell that no one can give like Karṇa.' It became an ideal for him. Like compulsive eaters, he became a compulsive giver. The reason was the pressure within to prove himself to be different, entirely different from others. The inner pressure that compelled him to give, also made him singularly responsible for the war. Even if Duryodhana wanted to listen to the elders' advice, it was Karṇa who refused to yield. He made sure that Duryodhana did not heed their advice.

So, I find in the *Mahābhārata*, each character has a particular emotional problem. In fact, the epic is a treasure trove of psychological study, a veritable gold mine. The variety of characters enacting their roles on the epic's vast canvas, reflect the depth of Vyāsa's knowledge of psychology. Each character is an archetype. You can understand from a study of these characters that history was made of emotions. Emotions make your life, and your family's life. Hence you cannot afford to be ignorant of the dynamics of emotional life.

EVERY PERSON IS AN EMOTIONAL BEING

It is unfortunate to hear people say that you should have emotions but not be emotional, that emotions are good but emotionalism is bad and so on. It is not a question of good or bad. People say that emotions are good but not emotionalism. Who is to decide? Everyone is emotional. Who is not emotional? You can turn on anybody.

Suppose someone says, "I am not emotional. I am a rational person," I can make him emotional in just three minutes. In fact, three minutes is too long.

I tell him or her, "No, no, you are emotional. I tell you, you are emotional."

"No, I am very dispassionate. Ask anybody."

"No, believe me, I know. Your father was emotional and so was your grandfather. In fact, your *gotra*, lineage, is emotional. It is not the non-emotional type at all."

Suppose I carry on with a few more lines, he will become emotional and say, "Don't bring my father into this."

Every person is an emotional being. Life is made of emotions. Emotions make marriages; they also break them. Emotions create sane people and insane ones too. Therefore, it is very important to understand the nature of the emotional person in you. It is this emotional person who makes or mars your life. When you look into the various forms of emotions, you find that they are merely different cuts of the same cloth; diverse manifestations of one single emotion which we call love.

LOVE IS THE BASIC EMOTION

Love is a dominant theme in music, particularly modern music. In our classical tradition, the Lord was the altar at which saints like Meera, Tyagaraja and others offered their devotion in various ways. In modern music, where rhythm is more predominant than musical content, the lyric is only about love, reciprocated love, rejected love or dejected love. A line typical of today's songs is "I love you this time, truly." Every lyric is about love, a love that is lost, that is hurt, that you yearn for. However, I cannot accept that this is how love is going to be because I am always going to talk of the thing I crave for. From the days of Adam, if that story is true, the problem has persisted. I want to be loved. The reason for this want is not far to seek. It is because I have no love for myself. It is the same reason why I feel ten feet tall when someone tells me that he or she loves me, that he or she accepts me as I am. It surprises me because how can anyone love me when I have no love for myself? Lack of self-love makes me turn away from myself. I cannot even stand a moment of loneliness. Even while waiting on the phone, I doodle to pass the time, to take my mind away from myself. The telephone service providers have understood this point so well that I now have music on hold. I cannot bear those few minutes, waiting for the other person to answer the phone, hence the music. I also misinterpret situations to validate my lack of self-love and as a result I suffer emotionally.

When somebody expresses love for me, I must have the nucleus, the emotional infrastructure to absorb that love. Similarly, in knowledge, I must have the intellectual framework, the cognitive ability to absorb knowledge, otherwise I am not going to understand what is being said or spoken. I should know in order to know. I should have in order to receive. If there is no self-love and self-acceptance, I cannot absorb love even if it is lavished on me. Consequently, when someone professes love for me, I constantly question and doubt the person. "Do you really love me? Why do you love me? How much do you love me?" The person has to invent stories to reply to my questions. What else can he or she do? If I continue, "Why do you love me?" The best I can expect is, "Because I am an idiot, that is why." There is no other answer, because there is no calculated love. Love is blind; it does not measure, demand or set agenda. Love is reckless; it gives all the way helplessly because it is the nature of love.

Lack of love for myself also makes me misunderstand love as control. I love the beautiful flower and at once my hands stretch out to pluck it. No one really knows what love is. So, love becomes control; at least for most of us it does. Most often the love of our parents is only control. It starts when the child is barely one month old. Since we only know to control, we cannot enjoy what we love because it is not possible to control situations. They do not always go the way we want and we find ourselves cheated. The story of love turns into a story of woes.

Every tragedy is unassimilated love, misunderstood love or obsessive love, be it Hamlet or Othello. You cannot afford to be ignorant of what love is. If you do not have an image of yourself, if you do not have love for yourself, love translates into control and consequently obsession. When someone accepts you for what you are, and declares his or her love for you, because it is the truth, that person becomes an object of your obsession, which is not healthy either. You need not change or control the person you love.

LOVE IS A PROFOUND WORD TO BE UNDERSTOOD

Love is not an ordinary topic that we understand. It is not what we read in magazines and novels. Love has become a commonplace and a much bandied about word. Some religions also profusely use this word, particularly the Televangelists in America who repeat in varying tones, "God loves you." What do they mean by this? God loves you and yet makes you suffer? Is God a sadist? What is this love? The God who loves you creates many viruses and continues to create newer and newer strains. Is it a sign of his love? It is more cruelty than love.

Another expression that is not understood is, God is love. If God is love, then what about hatred? Is that not God? If it is not, then poor God becomes completely inhibited and paralysed by hatred, anger and so on. We then call him almighty. There is no thinking, no understanding. Sometimes sentences can be misleadingly simple; we need to understand them properly. Such sentences are in fact very profound. There is *prasannatā*, simplicity, and more the *prasannatā* more the *gāmbhīrya*, profundity. So what appears simple is really very profound if it is from a person who knows. It is the prerogative of the well informed to be simple. Often, people hide behind big words to confuse others, because if the words are understood, their 'intellectual emptiness' will be exposed. Simple sentences are not to be taken lightly. 'God is love' or 'God loves you' need to be carefully studied and understood.

I thought the word 'love' should not be ignored and should be discussed thoroughly. It is not a prepared speech that I am going to unravel. I am going to explore along with you this great topic, a topic that makes your life meaningful. Life becomes wasted if this topic is not understood correctly. You seek something that is hard to find, and when you find it, you become secure and happy. Love is something that is hard to find.

Talk 2

Any Love is for My Sake

When someone says he or she is unhappy, it reveals something significant to me. It reveals that despite the vast expanding universe, the wonders of the world around, I can be unhappy. This is a desperate situation; even God will despair at the person's incapacity to be happy. When I explore the question of love, what does it mean to love, to be loving, I find that I am intimately, inextricably connected to the world. I am not apart from the world, a distant spectator; I am an active participant in the theatre of life. The various situations that I witness or participate in, are sources of constant amusement to me. Perhaps, this is the result when you explore and discover what is love, the meaning of the word love, *prema* in Sanskrit.

Yājñavalkya's teaching on love

Our scriptures discuss the topic of love, particularly the *Bṛhadāraṇyakopaniṣad*. Yājñavalkya, a well-respected great scholar, decided that he would retire to the forest to lead a contemplative life of a *sādhu*, a *sannyāsin*. When he took leave of his wife Maitreyī, she insisted on the reason for his leaving her. When he said it was for *mokṣa*, she questioned, "Will I get *mokṣa* with the wealth that you have given me?" Yājñavalkya, a truthful man, had to say, "*Vittena nāśā asti amṛtatvāya*, there is no way of gaining immortality by wealth."[2]

---

[1] *Bṛhadāraṇyakopaniṣad* 2.4.2

In this section of the *upaniṣad*, Yājñavalkya explores the root cause underlying all human pursuits such as wealth, power, pleasure and so on. He encourages Maitreyī, question by question, to discover the basic desire beneath all desires. He asks her to see if her desire is for wealth or for what wealth can bring. When she replies, he leads her with another question until she realises that it is love for the self that drives all human beings to do actions.

Love for the self, it is not the ordinary unhappy self that I am talking about. No one is interested in that. In fact, it is because of our unhappy self that we gossip, to get away from ourselves. We are only interested in the happy self, the self that is pleased, that is contented. Thus the *upaniṣad* analyses love and unfolds the vision of what love is, what every emotion is.

If we look at other life forms, emotions are more instinctive rather than deliberate. What makes a human being so unique is that he is the most self-conscious among the various living organisms on this planet. It gives him the capacity to be conscious of himself and a freedom to explore, to discover, to know, to choose, to feel and so on. Basically, a human being is cognitive. We call this capacity, *jñāna-śakti*. Psychology is born of this *jñāna-śakti*. Not only is a human being a conscious person, with a capacity to know, he is also a dynamically emotional person. He is endowed with a capacity to emote, to feel, which is *icchā-śakti*.

When a person appreciates another, it is cognitive, a form of both *jñāna-śakti* and *icchā-śakti*. The appreciation can turn into desire, a longing. Some call it 'love at first sight,' but this love belongs to a realm of fantasy. It is love of anticipation; he or she fantasises the object of love, what it would be to be with the person, how wonderful it would be and so on. The fact is, each person has a preconceived notion of the ideal 'other'. A man has his anima and a woman her animus. The person whom each one feels corresponds to their anima or animus, and that person becomes an object of love. A short euphoria, and the fantasy wears off. You find the person is not the ideal that you thought. The romance either ends in the couple drifting apart as each one wants to change the other to match the ideal.

Although a human being is cognitive, the emotional inhibits the cognitive person. The capacity to know is inhibited by certain emotional upheavals. Under such circumstances, even therapy does not help unless the person discovers a space between the emotional condition that is born of the unconscious and the adult person. That space, which is cognitive, has to be discovered. I have found my students, who were otherwise very brilliant, at sea when it came to facing themselves. The reason was the core person, the emotional person. Unless this problem is resolved, it is almost impossible to assimilate the vision of the *śāstra*. Further, in daily transaction, the cognitive person is completely overpowered and paralysed by the overwhelming emotions.

Emotions such as anger, *krodha*, completely deny wisdom. Anger dissipates whatever knowledge we may have. It is not just anger; any overwhelming emotion takes control of the person. It is not something unique to modern man.

It is an age-old problem. According to our *purāṇas*, sages and *yogins*, despite their erudition, used to get angry. They were also powerful people which made it worse. They could curse those who displeased them. Later, the very same person would also help to release his victim from the curse. From this we understand that before and after anger, the person is in control. It is only in between that anger takes control. It can happen to anybody. It is just that we have to pay attention to the emotions. Emotions and their nuances are many, but all of them have their basis in one emotion which is love.

The different forms of desires—to possess, to own, to experience, to win, to succeed—for various ends exist because there is an element of liking towards them. The word '*kāma*' reveals that the object of desire is fascinating, pleasing or going to please. The objects of your desire are objects of *kāma*. *Kāma* does not mean lust or passion as is commonly understood. It is love for the desired objects. Heading the list of desires, interestingly, is the husband and wife.

In the *Bṛhadāraṇyakopaniṣad* Yājñavalkya says[2] to his wife, you love your spouse, not for the sake of the spouse, but for your own sake. It is a very disconcerting idea that he or she does not love you but loves himself or herself. From this it is clear, love is something possible and it flows towards an object. The object of love is *ātma-śeṣa*, connected to you. Being connected to you, it is supposed to please you. If it pleases

---

[2] *na vā are patyuḥ kāmāya patiḥ priyo bhavati. ātmanastu kāmāya patiḥ priyo bhavati. na vā are jāyāyai kāmāya jāyā priyā bhavati. ātmanastu kāmāya jāyā priyā bhavati.* (*Bṛhadāraṇyakopaniṣad* 2.4.5)

you, it becomes an object of love and if it displeases you, it ceases to be an object of love. So, what you love is really that which brings out the pleased person in you.

Every person has a public face, certain form that is presented to the society. You have a persona, a mask, behind which the real person hides. There is lack of love and self-esteem. This lack drives you to be different from what you are, be it in clothes, profession, appearance or any other. Costumes and cosmetics are masks. In ancient India, the use of cosmetics, *alaṅkāra*, was meant to bring out the beauty within, like a beautiful painting on a good canvas. It was not considered a make up. You do not make up what you lack; you enhance what you have. You have a mask because you do not want people to know you completely. Even though you complain that no one understands you, you do not reveal yourself. How can others understand you, when you hide behind a mask? Sometimes the mask continues even in a relationship, like husband and wife.

MARRIAGE IS A PILGRIMAGE TO DISCOVER LOVE, TO GAIN MOKṢA

Marriage is an institution that we need, an institution where an individual completely bares himself or herself. It is a fusion of two egos. At the end of the Vedic marriage rituals, there are a few lines that read like a modern love story. *Hṛdayaṁ te dadāmi*, I give you my heart. *Tava cittam anucittaṁ bhavatu*, may our thoughts be in harmony. Both the partners have to enunciate these lines, otherwise one remains a noun while the other is reduced to an adjective. To make the other a nonentity is not marriage. Marriage between two individuals is a pilgrimage towards a common goal. Every human being is a pilgrim, really speaking. If you have a sacred goal you are pilgrim, if not you are a wanderer, a lost traveller with nowhere to go. At the end of the pilgrimage is the goal, *mokṣa*, a very profound word. It is really your own self-growth, self-discovery. In marriage *mokṣa* is the goal, with two pilgrims meaningfully coming together. This is symbolised by the seven steps, *saptapadi*: first step for prosperity, second step for progeny, third step for health, fourth and fifth steps for the health of both their parents, sixth step for friendship and finally the seventh step for *dharma*. The marriage is solemnised with this *saptapadi*. The *saptapadi* is followed by the *sakhya-homa*, a ritual for friendship. Please understand, friendship can exist only amongst equals. Friendship means equality; two equals marry each other. In our culture, age commands respect. The husband is usually older than the wife, naturally he is respected. Unfortunately, what started as respect has now turned into inequality, with the husband taking on the role of the master.

Marriage becomes a pilgrimage only when two equals join together because the sacrament of marriage is a means for an end; marriage is not an end in itself. If marriage is the ultimate end, it should be ideal; but what is ideal? Ideal means it should be custom made. Even if you specify, in detail, your requirements in a spouse, these requirements will change in time. Ideal marriage does not exist. If you enter marriage as the ideal end, it will end or if it does not; it will merely drag. Some people tell me, "Swamiji, we remain married because of our children." It is because they have not understood that marriage is not an end; it is a means to an end. If marriage is a means, then there cannot be a bad marriage. But both the people concerned should understand this. It will not work if only one partner understands. *Anucitta* is understanding. It is not an echo of the others' thoughts. Two persons with two different interests understand each other; it is *anucitta*. This is what we call love. It brings about a change in a person; makes him or her capable of trusting another. But as you grow old, you gradually discover distrust; trust becomes a casualty of growth. It is lack of trust that constantly makes you seek reassurance. I never saw my parents or grandparents discussing their relationship. But now I find couples have a need to discuss all the time about their relationship, their marriage. If two people love each other, and there is trust, what is there to discuss? Instead, it would be wonderful if they could start doing something together; it would be a work born of love. However, your capacity to trust is destroyed right from childhood.

You can relax only in trust. In distrust, there is suspicion, fear and anxiety. You have to be on guard all the time to ensure that you are not taken for a ride. You are forced to distrust and this is suffocating. Lack of trust is also the cause of people 'living' together and not marrying. They cannot trust themselves to a long-term commitment. This suffocation eases when you understand each other, when both egos fuse together. In understanding there is love. That is why marriage becomes an important institution for human emotional well-being.

Indian classical texts describe various types of marriages such as *gāndharva-vivāha, brāhma-vivāha, ārṣa-vivāha* and *paiśāca-vivāha*. In *gāndharva-vivāha*, personal choice is the predominant feature. The next two refer to marriages arranged by the families concerned. The *paiśāca* type refers to a marriage that is forced on an unwilling partner, abduction and so on. Whatever be the type of marriage, understanding is the fundamental ingredient for a successful marriage. Love becomes understanding. Without love you cannot understand; without understanding you cannot love.

LOVE FOR A THING IS FOR ONE'S SAKE

Yājñavalkya explains to his wife that love for yourself is expressed as love for the spouse; it is for your own sake and not for the sake of the other. You love an object, person or situation because it evokes the pleased you. Love is, therefore, the emotion that connects the pleased person and an external object. If an object evokes the displeased person, love turns to dislike. If love is for the object, then love must last as long as the object is, which it does not. The moment the object fails to bring out the pleased person, love vanishes and dislike or indifference sets in. Moreover, your poor self-image prevents you from accepting another's love. You have so many complexes in terms of your looks, hair, colour, qualification, wealth and so on. If mere looks can create complexes in you, where is the question of intellect and talent? When you are displeased with yourself, no matter what you achieve, you can never be pleased. Constant reassurance does not solve the problem at all. The other person will always come back with yet another why. When someone loves you, it means that he or she accepts the whole of you, including your appearance, hair, colour of skin, sense of dress, body, mind, emotion, intellect, knowledge, skills, and your limitations. You cannot love partially; you love the whole person. The fact that there is another person who loves you is wonderful. Someone in the world accepts you as you are, does not judge you, what more can you ask? The simple sentence, I love you, implies a complete acceptance of the other. In your acceptance, the other feels accepted. Despite the person's illness, complaints, feeling of lack, all of this and more, he or she is completely acceptable to someone. Nothing is comparable to this feeling. It is called relative love. I use the word relative to differentiate it from the absolute. You can now understand why love is so important for a healthy emotional life.

You cannot afford to underestimate the feeling of complete acceptance. Criticism, pointing out others' mistakes, these are our habits. In fact, the most commonly heard *mantra* today is, 'didn't I tell you?' Even when we go on holidays, pilgrimages, or organise events, the 'didn't I tell you' *mantra* relentlessly follows us. Didn't I tell you to bring water? Didn't I tell you to pack the woollens? Didn't I? Didn't I? In a cemetery there was a slab with the last words of John who was buried there. On the tombstone placed by his wife, the epitaph read, 'Didn't I tell you I was sick?' These were his last words. He is dead now because she did not listen to his 'didn't I tell you I was sick?' We can see why love is the least understood of emotions. There is love and trust but it is inhibited by our agenda for others. Let us try and understand love, relative or otherwise.

We saw earlier, love is always for whoever evokes the pleased person in you. In turn, you become an object of his or her love. For your happiness a person becomes beloved. Therefore, each should enrich and encourage the other. That is all what love is about. Love is for your sake alone, be it a person, an object or a situation.

You want to bring about a change in society, home, community and so on, it is all meant for you alone. People talk of selfless service. There is no such thing as selfless service. You cannot do any service without the self, the ego. Everyone has an ego. Sometimes, however, the self is confined to one's own body and mind and the person satiates his or her passions at the cost of others. Such a person is a self-centred person. Another can sacrifice his *rāgas* and *dveṣas*, likes and dislikes for the sake of his family, his children, their education and so on, because the family is his extended ego. The self has grown to include the family. Another person can give up for the sake of his community. He is sensitive to the needs of the community and feels that he cannot be happy if his community is unhappy. He cannot be like a slumlord living in luxury amidst dirt and squalor. It is not an intelligent way to live. A sensitive person would like the people around him to be healthy and the environment to be hygienic. He is able to identify his welfare with that of his community. This man's ego has extended beyond himself and his family. It has grown to include his community.

When we talk of selflessness it means that the person is more alive to the problems of the people around. It is not that the self is absent. It is a kind of community living, but can get out of hand if one is not careful. It is one thing to identify with one community, but quite another to incite one community against another. It is sheer opportunism for one to become a leader, political, social and so on. It rises out of selfishness and not selflessness. When you identify with a community, as I said earlier, your ego expands to include the community. From the individual, to the community, to the country, the nation, the culture, your ego can grow to include all of these and more. You can work for their growth and welfare. However, if you pit one against another, then pettiness steps in, and it becomes an ego trip. The self is very obviously present; bigger the self, more the dangerous, if there is no wisdom. For instance, you cannot neglect your family in the process of working for the country. You have to do both. You have to work within your limits and do whatever you are able to, let that be a satisfaction. Life is not all or nothing; it never is.

Therefore, even in the so-called selfless service, there is the self, the ego that has expanded to identify with the community, country and so on. If such a person does not work towards the welfare of the country, he or she will be miserable. But it is wrong to assume the role of a saviour. Even Kṛṣṇa could not prevent the *Mahābhārata* war. He could not convince Duryodhana despite all his wiles. You cannot change another. I thought that I could change people but in three months they made me realise that I cannot change anybody. However, if you want to change, nobody can stop you. You can try to cognitively change people; make them see. The more mature you are, you reach out to more and more people; it is natural. You do not wait for applause and recognition but do what needs to be done; although you must remember that through this service it is your own happiness that you seek.

If someone says, "I am doing selfless service," I ask,

"Why do you do it?"

"Oh, I want people to be happy."

"Why should they be happy? Let them be as they are."

"No, no, if they are unhappy, I will be unhappy."

"Oh, so you want to be happy. Your happiness is the reason for your work."

The central person in all this is only you. You are the pleased one. Vedanta starts from here.

Vedanta recognises the fact that love for various objects is only because they evoke the pleased you. Sometimes your love for something makes you unmindful of others' felicity, others' happiness. You are oblivious to them. You fight for things to evoke the pleased self. It is not the displeased self that you fight for. The displeased self is the one who is unhappy with the situation and wants to change the set up. The change can be simple changes such as rearranging the furniture at home, the carpet, the painting and so on. It is not for the sake of the furniture, it is only for your sake, *ātmanastu kāmāya.*

IS THE PLEASED SELF YOUR NATURE OR THE DISPLEASED SELF?

When the *upaniṣad* makes a statement, it is final. You cannot touch it. *Ātmanastu kāmāya sarvaṁ priyaṁ bhavati*–is a watertight statement. Vedanta begins right here. Is the pleased self your nature or is it the displeased self? It is a simple question but profound. If the displeased self is your nature and the pleased self appears now and then, you do not need Vedanta. It has nothing to offer that you do not know already. This is who you are, anyway. You do not learn anything. It is like a village schoolmaster who explains a text using the same words but a different tone, for example, father – faaather, mother – moooother, apple – aaaaappple and so on, and the child is not going to be any wiser. It is meaningless.

There are people who define life as a constant effort to bring in the pleased self more often than the displeased self. They have a few favourite lines of encouragement: "Life is like a fortune wheel; what goes up has to come down. When you are unhappy, wait it out for the wheel will turn." How will such lines help you? You know life is full of ups and downs, with more downs than ups. Restating what you already know will not help. It only makes you more frustrated. These are what I call as semi thinking, such as 'thought for the day,' 'words of wisdom' and so on. They do not help you; you just repeat them day after day and nothing happens. On the contrary, you develop a complex. "Oh, I should be like that but I am not. I am no good." Further, at home your partner waits to say, "Didn't I tell you so?" Such ideals are psychological calamities. They have destroyed humanity; have made us mediocre. Ideals have to be understood as such while the reality is different. People love ideals. They give in to them; they yield their thinking to the ideals. These sentences may have some truth, but the truth has to be discovered. "Why am I unable to face a problem? Why do I run away from difficulties? What should I do to face them?" This is what enquiry is. This is what Vedanta is. Please do not reduce Vedanta to few sentences.

Let us enquire if the displeased self is the real you. You know that two contradictory things cannot coexist. You cannot have a cold fire. Light and darkness cannot coexist in the same place at the same time. Two contradictory things cannot coexist, *viruddha-svabhāvatvāt*, being opposed to each other. Then how is it, you are both pleased and displeased? Why does the pleased person come now and then, while the displeased person is almost always there? Could the answer be, perhaps the pleased person is what you are and the displeased person is because you do not know what you are? Are you like that sugar cube, which longed to be sweet?

Let us suppose there was a sugar cube that had a human mind. It needs a human mind. It complained, "I am bitter. I want to be sweet."

I asked the sugar cube, "Do you want to be sweet today or tomorrow?"

The cube said, "I want to be sweet, today, tomorrow and the day after also."

" Do you want to be sweet all the time?"

"Yes, I want to be sweet all the time."

"Okay. Do you want to be sweet at home or outside home, inside the container where you are or outside the container?" A container is its home. In the world, there are only two places, inside the home and outside.

The sugar cube said, "I want to be sweet both inside and outside."

Next, I asked, "Do you want to be sweet sitting by the side of the chilly powder or the tamarind sauce?"

It said, "I do not care who is a around me, I want to be sweet. Related to all of them I want to be sweet."

What does it mean? There is no other way except to be already sweet. If it wants to be sweet at all times and at all places, sweetness must be its nature.

"Do you want to be happy today or tomorrow?"

"I want to be happy always."

"Do you want to be happy at home or outside?"

"I want to be happy everywhere."

All the questions that I asked the sugar cube, I could ask you, and your answers will not be any different. It means that you should be happy now for it is your nature. Maybe that pleased person whom you come across now and then is exactly what you are. "How come I do not know?" I will counter that question, "How come you do not know? How come you do not know your own nature?" You need Vedanta to answer these questions.

TALK 3

I AM THE PLEASED SELF

In the vision of the Veda, what you really love is not an object or a person outside, but yourself alone. You love yourself, the self that is pleased. Consequently, if an object outside pleases you, makes you more secure or more happy than what you are, then it becomes an object of your love. If you love the pleased self, then at the same time you must recognise the dislike you have towards the displeased self, the displeased you. You do not like to be discontented with yourself. Of these two, the pleased and the displeased you, which is the real one? It is similar to the dual behaviour of a quantum object. It is both a wave and a particle depending on how you observe it. If you wish to measure the velocity it is a wave, and a particle, if you wish to pinpoint its position. The self also appears to have a dual nature, pleased and displeased.

When you review your life, you find that by and large it is the displeased self that operates. The pleased self appears briefly and disappears as quickly as it came. No sooner you discover you are happy, happiness passes. Is it not natural for you to assume that the displeased self is the real you? Any pleasure or happiness you experience, perhaps is an epiphenomenon, an adventitious occurrence at a given time that passes away. As far back as you can remember, you have always been a wanting person, as a child, as a teenager, and as an adult.

Who amongst us who did not want to score hundred percent in every subject matter, come first in every sports event? Who did not want to score sixes off every ball in an over? Who did not want to be the greatest bowler, the greatest batsman or the greatest soccer player? We only fantasised but we could never accomplish. The parents thought their child would be a genius. As the child grew, they also edited their ambitions for their child. They constantly revised and edited their vision of an Einstein or Newton and settled for something less. Our wants remained, many of them unfulfilled. Finally, we always settled for something less.

There is nothing wrong in our desires. Desiring is a human privilege. An animal does not have this privilege. A cow does not ask the bullock, "Honey, shall we eat Chinese or Indian tonight?" Desires are endowed to us and should not be looked upon as liabilities. They are expressions of the *icchā-śakti*. Emotions and desires are manifestations of this power.

However, desires do not remain as privileges. They become wants that demand fulfilment and unless you fulfil them you feel you have not achieved, you are not successful. Of course, you could not fulfil many of them; your life is replete with unfulfilled desires. You could go so far as to say that these unfulfilled wants constitute the individual.

If you are a wanting individual, it is understandable. Yet in spite of these various desires that keep you wanting, occasionally you also find yourself happy. It is not peculiar to any given individual; everyone has his or her moments of joy, however few or far in between they may be. Here again, you have a dual phenomenon. You are generally unhappy with occasional moments of happiness. It is a contradiction in terms. Those who have inquired into happiness have drawn certain conclusions. You become happy when you fulfil a desire. It means happiness lies in between the fulfilment of a desire and the rise of another. It also means that if you do not have any desire, you will be very happy. We need to analyse this conclusion.

HAPPINESS IS NOT AN OBJECT NOR AN ATTRIBUTE

The experience of happiness appears to be adventitious, an event that has happened in my life. The displeased seems to have become happy. If that is so, I should see what made me happy. One thing I know is that there is no object in the world called happiness. There are many objects in the world, the sun, stars, moon, mountain, cow, eagle, apple, potato, man, woman and so on but I do not see an object called happiness. If happiness is not an object, perhaps it is an attribute, adjective to an object. For instance, green is not an object but is an attribute to an object, a green leaf or green apple. Similarly, although there may not be a substantive called happiness, there can be an adjective, an attribute to a substantive, a happy substantive. I have seen a green leaf, a bitter fruit, a sweet orange but I have never seen a happy object, happiness sticking to an object.

One American asked me, "Swami why can't we say happy Dayananda?" I replied, "Happy Dayananda? How do you know I am happy? You are making an inference. May be it is part of my training to appear happy. And when I go to my room, I bury my head in the pillow and cry. How do you know that I am happy?" As I inquire into what is happiness, I find that happiness is not an adjective, much less is it a noun. Please understand this well. By dismissing the substantive and the attribute, I have covered the entire world. What is left out is time.

HAPPINESS IS NOT A PARTICULAR TIME OR PLACE

Is there a particular time when you become happy? The clock strikes and at once you become happy and a little later, you become unhappy. Is it true? No, you can be happy any time. In the West there is a 'happy hour' when the pubs sell drinks at a small discount. This is just after office hours so that people can drop in on their way home. I consider it the unhappiest hour. So, there is no particular time you become happy and no particular place you become happy. You may think heaven is such a place where you can be happy. It is not true; you can be unhappy even in heaven. In fact, you will definitely be unhappy there because there are comparisons, varying degrees of comfort. This is the description of heaven.

HAPPINESS IS NOT WITHIN

No particular place is happiness; no particular time is a source of happiness; no substantive, no object can be called happiness. Happiness can never be an attribute to a substantive. If that is so then what makes you happy whenever you are happy? You may say, 'happiness is within.' It is another myth. Is happiness within? What does within mean?

Is it the liver, heart or kidney? Organs cannot feel happiness, so it must be the mind. Does that mean there is no mind when you are sad? In fact, sadness requires a lot of thinking. Therefore, you cannot say the mind makes you happy.

ONE IS HAPPY EVEN WITHOUT FULFILLING A DESIRE

There is another option and that is, happiness lies between the fulfilment of one desire and the rise of another. That is also not totally true because sometimes you fulfil a desire and wish that you were never born. You fulfil a long drawn desire and find that you are not happy. Further, you also find that you can be happy without fulfilling a desire. You read a story or hear a joke and you laugh. The correlation between happiness and the fulfilment of a desire is at best variable.

Two friends bought a horse each. They had a few acres of land and they allowed the horses to graze there. One friend asked the other, "How do we know which horse is mine and which is yours?"

The other friend suggested, "Why don't you paint your horse with some stripes?"

The other man agreed and painted his horse with stripes. However, a month later, the rains washed away the stripes. Again they had problems identifying their horses.

"Now what shall we do?"

"Cut the mane on your horse. The one without the mane is yours."

The man cut the mane of his horse, but it grew back again, and the problem remained. Next, he cut the tail but that also grew back. Then, the other friend had a bright idea. He said, "Why not do it this way, the white horse is yours, the brown is mine." (Laughter).

Did you fulfil a desire now? Has your circumstances changed at home or the office? Yet all of you laughed. Can you not see the logic? If, in spite of your wants you are happy occasionally, it only proves the point that you need not fulfil desires to be happy. This leaves you the possibility that perhaps you are the very happiness. Whenever you are happy now and then, it is this happiness that you come across, although you attribute it to some other source.

It is similar to a dog while chewing a dry bone cuts its mouth. It tastes its own blood and attributes it to the juiciness of the bone. It thinks, "Before I ate the bone there was no blood. Only now I taste blood. So it must be the juicy bone." So too when you listen to music you are happy, and you attribute the happiness to the music. Before listening to the music you were not happy but while listening you are happy. Therefore, music must be the source of happiness. This is your logic. However, the music that you listen to is a source of unhappiness to your son who prefers contemporary music. So the same music is a source of happiness for you and unhappiness for your son. Therefore, you cannot cite it as a cause for happiness. You commit the same error of attributing happiness to the object of your experience.

There are some who say the world is a trap; it does not make you happy. On the contrary, it makes you unhappy.

This also is not true. The world does make you happy. Look at the stars, the beauty of nature, the world of music, thousands of examples to prove that the world makes you happy. Here, our *śāstras* come to your help. They categorically state that happiness is your nature. The happiness that you experience is exactly what you are. It is what you are. It does not exclude the world, your body, mind or senses. Despite your mind and senses being very much present, you are happy. Your next question could be, "When I am unhappy, what am I?" Well, let us look at these two experiences and see which is the one that you love to be.

HAPPINESS IS YOURSELF ALONE

What is natural is not a matter for complaint. That I have hunger, thirst and so on, is not a matter for complaint; it is natural. That I sleep every night is not a problem. No one complains, "Oh, I have to sleep every night. I do not know why, but I sleep at night." It is not a matter for complaint. It is, however, a matter for complaint if I do not get sleep.

If my eyes do not see, my ears do not hear or if I have no appetite, these are all matters for complaint. The reason is because it is not natural. If the sun is bright, tamarind is sour or sugar is sweet, it is their nature to be so. Similarly, that I am happy is not a cause for complaint. If I am unhappy, however, it is definitely something to complain about. I worry about my unhappiness. I look for solace and comfort from people. I seek diversion from myself. In fact, according to the modern measure of success, the more diversions I have, the more successful I am. I can understand clearly that unhappiness is not acceptable, even though it is part of my life. Whenever I am unhappy, I always try to be different. Equally, if someone else is unhappy, I reach out and try to relieve the sorrow. However, when someone is happy I do not offer my condolences. It is a welcome state and most acceptable. Therefore, to be happy is as natural a commitment as it is to be away from being unhappy.

Our *śāstras* tell that the happiness that you experience is yourself alone, which is why you love to be happy, not now and then but all the time and at all places. Unless it is your own nature, you cannot accomplish that. In the vision of the *śāstras* you are that happiness. Happiness is an experiential word. A better definition would be, freedom from the sense of limitation, freedom from the sense of want, freedom from the attempt to become, and it is this freedom, *mokṣa*, which is your nature, which is you. The *śāstras* reveal the self to be the very thing that you love. What you love is fullness, the freedom from limitation. Let us call it *pūrṇatva*. This *pūrṇatva*, fullness, is exactly what you seek and it is you.

While there is every reason for you to feel small and insignificant, in the vision of the *śruti* you are the whole. If you look at yourself from the scheme of things called the *jagat*, you cannot but see yourself as an insignificant entity. Equally, there is reason for you to say that you are the whole. What is the reason? It is the shift in your vision. I would like you to understand clearly that a point of view is not the view. Only if the view is clear, a point of view is possible.

Without a complete picture, you cannot have a point of view. For instance, I see an 'abstract painting. Unable to understand the painting, I ask the artist, "What is the significance of this painting?" He points to the title written below, 'Perspective of a table.' I turn to him, "It doesn't look like a table." He explains, "Swami, when I lie down on the floor and look up at the table, this is how it looks." For the artist it is a perspective because he knows the full view of the table. A perspective is not a perspective if the total view of the object is not known. A spare part of a machine is not a meaningful part if the whole scheme is not understood. Your point of view is that you are small and insignificant but you do not know the whole view of who you are. When the whole vision is not clear, how do you come to this conclusion? From a point of view it does appear that you are small, insignificant and so on. We have seen that earlier. Now, let us try and understand what the whole view is and whether your conclusion is correct.

YOU ARE THE WHOLE

If there is something that includes everything, encompasses everything, we can call it *pūrṇa*, the whole. Will this *pūrṇa* exclude you? If it does, can it be the whole? Should not the whole include you? It should include you; it can never be separate from you. This is what you experience in a moment of happiness. When you listen to music, you are happy. The music, the mind and you are there. There is no wanting-wanted situation. It is the situation where the wholeness is experienced. You do not lack the experience of the whole; you need to understand the experience of the whole. Please see the difference. You experience the whole whenever you are happy. You can never be away from the whole.

When you look at me, I become an object of your consciousness. What is the distance between consciousness and the object that you are conscious of? Is there a distance? You are conscious of space. Space is the object of your consciousness. Between space and consciousness is there a distance? If there is a distance, what causes that distance? Is it space? Space, as I said, is already an object of consciousness. The object space is never away from consciousness.

The universe is not separate from consciousness. In fact, you are unlike everything else in the sense, everything else is the object of consciousness. Space, time, earth, sun, moon, any object, micro or macro, is object of consciousness. Any subject matter is an object of consciousness. The numerous forms, the different colours, the sounds of various frequencies, flavours, tastes, concepts and ideas, everything is object of consciousness; the objects are variable. What is invariable is only consciousness. In Sanskrit we call this consciousness *samvit* or *cit*. This is what you experience when you are happy. It is the same consciousness that you experience when you are unhappy, although you do not know it.

You are unlike anything else

Despite my explanation, the problem of being small does not disappear. The smallness is really not a problem, if you are the only being on the planet with no one to compare.

The problem arises only when you compare yourself with another and find yourself falling short. Being self-conscious, you compare, and comparisons cause complexes. Further, comparisons are only with people, and not with other dissimilar objects or beings. You do not compare yourself with a rock or a tree. You can be jealous only of another human being. A great musician compares himself to a rock star and not to a rock. Compared to a rock star, he envies the other's popularity, wealth and success. It is comparison with the similar that causes complexes.

Our *śāstras* prod you to question the object of your comparison. As you analyse you will find that everything else in this world is unlike you. Every object, be it time, space, quasars, quarks, individuals, anything that you come to know inferentially, presumptuously or directly through your own senses or with instruments, is an object of your consciousness. When I say everything, it also includes concepts such as heaven, hell, and so on; they are all objects of consciousness. You are the only source of consciousness; the rest are objects of your consciousness.

You have pronouns in every language. The second person pronoun is you which can be used to any number of people. The third person pronoun, he, she or it, can be used for any number of men, women or objects. However, when it comes to the first person pronoun I, in how many places can you use the word? What is the locus of I? Is there a second place that you can use I? There is only one locus and that is you, for there is no second I. There is no second consciousness. It means everything is unlike consciousness. So, you have nothing to compare with. You are like yourself. There is no one like you. The object of consciousness, which is unlike you, is not separate from that consciousness. It does not have an existence apart from consciousness.

Anything, you think of, is in your consciousness, whether it is a concept of beauty, an aesthetic sense, a sentiment, it is never away from consciousness. Your dream is in consciousness. Your sleep is in consciousness. All these are but consciousness. It is the wholeness of the self that is you. This is the view, understand, the whole view. The point of view is with reference to a specific, your body for instance. You can say you are limited with reference to your body. With reference to your knowledge, to anything you can say, you are limited. With reference to yourself, you are free from limitation. There is a reason for you to be happy because it is what you are. You cannot avoid being happy, despite all the limitations. Even the most miserable person smiles at times. Sometimes, I find some people in the audience very serious, trying hard not to laugh. Often they become my challenge and I see them finally laughing.

In spite of all the tragedy and sorrow, you do come across yourself. That is what happens when something captures your imagination–a purple moment, something beautiful, a sentence, a phrase, a colour, an arrangement, innocent laughter of a child, and at that time the wanting 'you' is drowned. It is due to grace that you can suspend your memory and for the moment the wanting you is forgotten. You have to make an effort to remember the wanting you. The real you, the joyous you, like the sun, reveals itself at such moments.

You find that you and the world have become one whole. It is the wholeness that you experience when you are happy, because the nature of the self, the *ātman*, is happiness. The self is unlike anything else. Referred by the word 'I,' the self becomes the centre of all your experiences.

Talk 4

The 'I' is limitless

You find in the world, there are only two things to begin with, I, the subject and everything else, that is not–I. When you look into what is 'I' and 'not–I' the obvious line of division is the skin, the extremities of your body. Beyond the skin is not–I. The shirt you wear, though close to your body, is not–I. It is your shirt but not you. The *śāstra* questions this. The physical world is an object and exists because you have a means of knowing it. You cannot say that it exists unless you know it. When you say 'this is,' you have a valid means of knowledge to prove the existence. So what you say exists is what you objectify by one of the means of knowledge.

Let us apply the same principle to a pot, *ghaṭa-draṣṭā ghaṭād bhinnaḥ*, the knower, the seer of a pot, is distinct from the pot. A pot is because you are conscious of it. It is an object of your consciousness. Anything that becomes an object of your knowledge can be said differently. Therefore, when you say 'pot is,' it can be said as 'pot consciousness is.' Pot has already become an object of your consciousness, of your knowledge. So too a flower is, flower consciousness is. Swami is, Swami consciousness is. Time is, time consciousness is. Anything is, that object consciousness is. If this is so, your physical body also is not an object outside your consciousness. It is only your relationship with it that differs.

ERROR OF TAKING NOT-I AS I

The manner of my relating and the reality of the object do not change. For example, there are many houses and one of them is my house. There are many people and one of them is my father. There are many bodies and one of them is my body. In all the above examples, it is clear that I have an intimate relationship with one and not with the others of the same category. This is my house and that is not. This is my father and the other is not. This is my body and the others are not. It is clear. I am intimately connected to and related to my physical body even though it is an object of consciousness. There is an obvious confusion. I do not look upon my body as an object of consciousness. Instead, I look upon it as myself.

Consequently, I identify myself with the conditions of my body in terms of appearance, weight, mortality and so on. By identifying with the physical body, I also identify with its functions as well as with the mind and senses. I know that there is hunger, thirst. There is hunger consciousness and thirst consciousness, but I say it differently, 'I am hungry or I am thirsty.' Equally, when I look at myself from the standpoint of the senses, if there is no sight or hearing, I say, 'I am blind or I am deaf,' even though blindness or deafness is something you are conscious of. They are objects of your consciousness. This confusion arises only because of my identity with my physical body, mind and senses. Therefore, I refer all these as 'I,' although they are objects of my consciousness.

When I say object, I mean the grammatical object. It is an object of consciousness. When I say, 'I am blind or I am deaf,' I cannot say so without 'seeing,' without being aware of my blindness or deafness. I see that I do not see. So blindness is an object of my consciousness, like those mentioned earlier.

The conclusion, 'I am blind or I am deaf,' is based upon the experience of the person; that is, the conclusion is the experience, or the experience is the conclusion. Either way it is a conclusion. There is experience of not seeing and the conclusion is, 'I am blind.' There is experience of not hearing and the conclusion is that 'I am deaf.' The conclusion of my mind is my condition. The emotion prevailing in the mind at a given time is my condition at that time, like I am angry or I am jealous and so on.

Thus, I assume the condition of my mind and the mind keeps changing. The truth here is, the mind changes all the time while I remain constant. The self, the I, identifies with the varying conditions of the mind. So the angry I is now the understanding I, the accommodating I, the loveable I. The confused I is the clear I now, the hesitant I is the decisive I, the forgetting I is the remembering I.

So too my memory is an object of consciousness, my emotion is an object of consciousness, my knowledge is an object of consciousness, my ignorance is an object of consciousness. Yet I say, 'I am both knowledgeable and ignorant.' It is amazing. Though it is true it depends on the standpoint from which the I say, I am knowledgeable and ignorant. I am knowledgeable with reference to what I know and ignorant with reference to what I do not not know.

Similarly, I am a liker with reference to what I like and conversely a disliker with reference to what I do not. It appears the 'I' can be viewed from different standpoints, but it is only a point of view.

With reference to the body I am tall, short, old or young. From the standpoint of *prāṇa* I am hungry, thirsty, healthy or otherwise. From the standpoint of the mind, I am restless and so on. These are all standpoints.

I can also look at myself differently with reference to the people connected to me. To my father I am either son or daughter, and to my children, I become mother or father. Each one of them is a point of view.

'I' IS INVARIABLE CONSCIOUSNESS

The question now is, what or who are you? A point of view becomes clear only when the view, the vision is clear. If the view is not clear, the point of view becomes the view. It is confusing because it is variable. That which is invariable in all the points of view is I, *aham*. What is I? It is consciousness. It cannot be but self-revealing consciousness.

Anything you objectify implies knowledge. It implies the presence of consciousness which is present invariably. When you say I am, the I is invariable and consciousness is invariable. Are there two things, consciousness and I? No. It is the invariable consciousness which is referred by the word I. Consciousness joins every situation. With sleep you say sleep consciousness. With dream it is dream consciousness. With waking, it is waking consciousness. With any object, it is that object consciousness. The objects and situations vary but consciousness is constant; it is invariable all the time. This is the real meaning of the word 'I'. Therefore, when you say, 'I am,' you are saying consciousness is. If this is so, then nothing is totally opposed to consciousness. This is the next step in understanding. Nothing is outside or separate from consciousness.

TWO ORDERS OF REALITY

You cannot separate an object from consciousness, in the sense, when object is, consciousness is, when the object is not, consciousness still is. If A is there, then B is there. If B is not there, A is still there. It is two orders of reality. Let us take a pot made of clay. So, pot is, clay is. Now think of a pot without any material, like clay, metal or any other. If not a pot, let us imagine a shirt without a material. Imagine anything without its material. It is amazing how people miss the obvious. You say it is a clay pot. It is linguistically correct except that clay becomes an adjective to pot, whereas the word pot does not really have an object. The weight of the pot is the weight of clay. It feels like clay. In fact, I could say, there is only clay. Pot is not space; it is neither of clay nor in clay. Then, what is this pot? This is Indian magic. There is no pot; there is only clay.

However, you cannot dismiss a pot as non-existent. It has its uses; it holds water. So a pot has to be given a status in terms of its ontological status. The pot was a possibility that was collapsed by the pot maker. Collapsing a possibility is to actualise it. Pot is a form and that form alone is the meaning of the word, pot. Form is not a substance; it is only an attribute.

If pot is not a substance and it is an attribute to clay, you should call it potty clay and not clay pot. In potty clay, pot becomes an adjective which is the correct term because clay is the substance; it is *satya*. Pot is definitely *mithyā*. *Mithyā* is not delusion or illusion or false. It is a reality. It has a form and a function. It is what we say, Bhagavān's *sṛṣṭi*, creation.

If clay is the substance, can you say that the pot is an attribute? No, simply because pot-ness, the nature of pot, is not intrinsic to clay. Every time you think of clay, you do not think of pot, is that not true? A pot is of clay and so is a plate, a lid or a cup. There are many forms but one clay. You can have a million pots but if you count clay, you have counted all of them. *Ekasmin vijñāte*, with the knowledge of one, everything else is as well known because the substance is only one and everything else is form and function. In terms of reality it is only one.

We have these two orders of reality. One is without being a pot, a chain and so on. Clay is without being a plate or a pot. Gold is without being a chain or a ring. However, a golden chain is gold; golden bangle is gold; golden anything is gold. In other words B is A while A is not B. It is an amazing reality. It makes the difference in life because A happens to be you while B happens to be everything else. Think of anything and it is sustained by consciousness, such as space consciousness, time consciousness and so on. There is no distance between consciousness and the object. Further, while consciousness is free from all objects, objects are not free from consciousness. It is consciousness which is the nature of *ātman*, I. Consciousness has no form or parts, it is dimension free. Consciousness is spatially free. Consciousness is not in space, whereas space is consciousness; it is in consciousness. Consciousness is what you experience every time you are happy.

CONSCIOUSNESS IS SATCITĀNANDA

Consciousness is not bound by space or time. If you look at the nature of time, it is a strange phenomenon. When you think of the past, you are thinking of the past right now. Can you think of the past in the past? No, you think of the past right now. Similarly, you think of the future, right now. 'Now' is the reality of time. If you look into what is now, does it imply a length of time? No, because every length is subject to further and further divisions. If you take a minute, it has sixty seconds. A second has one million microseconds. A microsecond has one million picoseconds. You can keep dividing until there is no length of time. Then, what is now? You think of time, time consciousness is. You look into time, the content is consciousness, length free consciousness, neither spatially limited nor time-wise limited. Therefore, consciousness is *sat*, *cit* and *ānanda*. *Ānanda* is limitlessness; it is not bliss. If you say bliss, it becomes experiential and you will be waiting for that bliss forever.

THE VISION OF THE WHOLE IS COMMUNICABLE

When you use words such as bliss, communication stops. All of you have the experience of some kind of bliss, ice cream bliss, music bliss, disco bliss and so on. This *ātmā* bliss is the best of them all! Often, you find the word bliss written with a capital B or all the letters in capitals. It only leads to confusion and there is no communication. Whereas the knowledge of the whole is entirely communicable. It is our teaching tradition. There is nothing mystic about it.

A mystic cannot create another mystic. If a mystic has certain experience of some underlying harmony in the world, he cannot make the other person have a similar experience. He can only say something. If he has a means to communicate his vision, then there is nothing mystic about his experience. In our teaching tradition, there is a *paramparā*, *guru-śiṣya-paramparā*, teacher-student lineage. The teaching can be passed on.

We employ words that are chosen carefully. They should make you see. Of course, words have limitations and we should be aware of them. We create a situation from where you have no choice but to see. This is what the teaching is about. For example, if you wish to point out a particular star or any celestial object to someone, it is difficult to point with your finger. So, you choose a tree or a building and lead the person from there. First you point out a tree, then lead him to a branch and from there to its tip. "Now next to that tip, do you see the bright star?" His excited exclamations speak for themselves. This is how the teaching takes the student through, to understand the vision. It is how the vision is communicated. Since the subject is you, I have to only create a situation like the branch of a tree and help you recognise that limitlessness is the nature of the self, it is not limited by time or by space.

LOVE IS WHOLENESS MANIFEST

You believe that you are the body and therefore you are subject to *trividha-pariccheda*, three-fold limitations: *deśataḥ*, spatially, *kālataḥ*, time-wise and *vastutaḥ*, object-wise. When you say you are limited, you are wanting, you are useless and so on, it is the body or mind's limitation that you identify with. It is due to error that is born of ignorance. The *śāstra* corrects this error.

From the standpoint of the physical body, it is good that it is not limitless. If it is, how are you going to get up? The truth is 'I am' is limitless. And the problem is also centred on this I and not elsewhere. The body has no complexes, you have complexes. The mind also does not have any problem, although the mind is generally everybody's whipping boy. Mind is only an instrument, *antaḥ-karaṇa*. The problem is the individual, you, who has every form of complex: 'I am fat, I am useless, I am a failure.' Fortunately, the truth is, 'I am' limitless consciousness which is *ānanda*. From a point of view, the limitless 'you' has a limited body, limited mind, senses, but it is not a problem. It is like the actor A playing the role of beggar B. A is B while B is not A. Similarly, despite the limitation of the body, mind and senses, you are free from the sense of limitation because you know what the 'I' is.

Knowing the truth of I, you are free enough to have a limited body, a limited mind, and limited senses. This is the freedom and it is the nature of the self. It is this self that you love. The love is for the pleased self which it already is. But because of your wrong conclusions about yourself you struggle to be happy. Thanks to some grace, you find yourself in a situation where the wanting you is suspended for the time being. It is the greatest grace when you are able to suspend the dissatisfied I in moments of happiness.

It is the same happiness that you discover in love. When someone says, "I love you," you accept yourself for the time being through the eyes of the other. He or she totally accepts you which is why love seems to express happiness and joy. At that time there is complete suspension of this wanting, smarting self. The petty person is given up for the moment because of an overwhelming experience like music, a joke, of something beautiful, or something profound. It captures you and you find that you are the whole. This is happiness which you experience in different degrees. *Ānanda*, happiness is manifest as love when related to an object. Love is a dynamic form of wholeness, the *ātman*. Wherever there is love, there is wholeness. You love the wholeness through another object that brings you wholeness. It makes you discover some wholeness about you. Therefore, that object becomes an object of love.

RAMIFICATIONS OF LOVE

Love undergoes different ramifications. It becomes compassion when the object of love requires consideration, some consolation or help from you, and you respond because that person deserves help. From compassion, love turns into service. It creates a condition within you to help you understand yourself. There can be love only where there is understanding, otherwise love cannot sustain. You may marry because you love someone, or marry and discover love later. Either way, marriage will be rewarding only if there is understanding. Love is the basis for understanding.

Love is only when you free yourself from your agenda for the other. Unless you drop your agenda, you cannot understand another. Love paves the way for this understanding. Unfortunately, we do not understand what love is, not even relative love. In absolute terms love is *ānanda*. It is a manifest form of *ātman*, the wholeness of *ātman* which is why love accommodates, because it is whole. Since it accommodates, any omission or commission on the part of the other does not cause concern.

Lack of understanding turns love into obsession. When this happens, love not only gets hurt, it also causes hurt. You are supposed to rise in love and not fall in love, as is the commonly used expression. It has become a money spinning theme these days, commercialised to such an extent that love is nothing but a bubble, a make believe bubble. Without understanding, love becomes obsessive and can also turn into hatred. When you cannot control the object of your love, you begin to dislike the very object that you profess to love. In extreme cases, the hatred can even lead to murder. You destroy that which you love. Love is now hatred. In fact, there is no such thing as hatred. It is only unfulfilled love, love that has gone sour.

Jealousy also is love. When someone gets the thing that you love and want, you become jealous. It is called as *dṛṣṭi*, evil eye and so on, in Sanskrit it is called *mātsarya*. In the *Gītā*, this emotion, *mātsarya*, is specifically mentioned. When talking about a *jñānin*, a wise person, he is said to be *vimatsara*, free from jealousy. In Sanskrit jealousy is defined as anguish at others' success, particularly if that success is conjoined with your failure. Jealousy is another ramification of love and is the most illegitimate of emotions.

Anger also is love. When your love for something is thwarted or denied, you are hurt and there is pain. It is this pain, *duḥkha*, which manifests as anger. Anger is not pain of the present. It is always some old pain manifesting. The current situation merely evokes the latent feeling. Everyone has his or her erroneous zone, vulnerable area. There is already buried pain inside. All it requires is a trigger, someone to touch the button, and there is an outburst. You need to be aware of yourself; you need an insight into your inner world.

There is only one emotion which is real, which is your nature, and that is love—love as compassion, sympathy, understanding, giving, yielding, and as friendliness also. People often say, "You should be friendly, you should be accommodating, you should be this and that." It is not a question of should or should not; it is what you are. You do not ask a sugar crystal to be sweet; its nature is to be sweet. You are misled to have ideals without understanding that these are not ideals; these are you, your nature. It is a question of understanding; it is not to be commanded or demanded. People are mediocre, mediocre not in their professions or achievements, but in their living. It is not that they are incapable of living intelligently; it is just that they are misled. Compassion is your nature, as is sympathy, and empathy; it is the key that unlocks these emotions.

Empathy is not the prerogative of a special heavenly individual. It is a natural human trait. When you see any suffering, you pick up the pain. It is empathy. I often give the example of a tennis match. On the television you can watch clearly the expression on the faces of the two players. When the winner comes up to the net to shake hands with the opponent, after a hard won final, he picks up the disappointment of the other. His earlier ecstasy is quickly replaced by sympathy for the other's defeat. It is empathy. The world enters you through empathy and invokes compassion. Compassion, in turn, moves you to act, to reach out and help.

Even as compassion wells up in you, you come up with reasons why you cannot help. The so called practical you quickly overwhelms the natural you. First you are human, only then you are a practical, pragmatic human. Returning to empathy, it is so very evident in your encounter with people begging at the traffic lights. If a begging person asks, with dignity, "Please give me some money sir, I have not eaten for days." you will probably not give him a second of your time. However, if he should plead, pester and beseech you, "Sir, sir, sir, food sir, hungry sir, not eaten sir," you will definitely give him something. The man knows the psychology of begging. He makes you feel so wretched and you cannot stand the pain. So, you give him something to ease your pain. He evokes your empathy.

TALK 5

GAINING ELIGIBILITY FOR KNOWLEDGE

The essential nature of the self is wholeness; it lacks nothing. Basically, you want to be, to live. Everyone wants to live; nobody wants to die. There is a love to be. Then there is love for freedom. In other words, there is love for freedom from the limitation of time. You want to be timeless, full, complete and whole. You cannot stand a sense of incompleteness, of lack. Then you cannot stand ignorance; there is the need to know. If you want to make your partner lose his or her sleep all you have to do is to say :

"I have something important to tell you, but you should not tell this to anyone."

"Okay. What is it?"

"Oh, it is too late now. I will tell you tomorrow."

That is it. The whole night, the person will wonder who it is about, what and why. Sleep has vanished for the night.

The love to know expresses itself even in the desire to read the gossip weeklies. You want to know everything that is happening around you. You are hurrying to your office. On the way you see a small crowd on the pavement. You stretch your neck out to see what is the cause. This is what they call rubber necking. Two people are in deep conversation. As you walk past, you cannot help slowing down. Your entire attention is behind the ear; even your head bends slightly, to get the gist of their conversation. It arises from the basic love to know. You cannot bear being ignorant.

If I have to describe the basic urge of a self-conscious being, it would be in one sentence, that you want to live a day more, happily, without being ignorant. To live a day more reveals the desire for eternity, timelessness that is the nature of the self. Your desire to be free from ignorance arises from the notion that you are ignorant. Please note the word notion. It is not the truth; it is your notion. In fact, you are neither ignorant nor knowledgeable, for you are ignorant with reference to what you do not know and knowledgeable with reference to what you know. You are *cit*, consciousness, which makes you aware of both ignorance and knowledge. You are also aware of the need to be free from any sense of limitation. Fullness is your nature which is the reason why you want to be happy.

ANY KNOWLEDGE PRESUPPOSES ELIGIBILITY

Knowledge is freedom from ignorance. Knowledge here is knowledge of yourself, of your nature. Self-knowledge, like any other knowledge, presupposes certain eligibility. It requires certain factors. If you wish to see an object you require certain factors—light, the object, eyes capable of sight and the mind behind the eyes. If all these factors are present definitely you will see the object. Even if I ask you not to see the object, you cannot help yourself. You will definitely see. Knowledge does not depend on your permission or your will. It takes place if the requisites are fulfilled. Be it sight, smell, taste, touch or sound, knowledge will take place.

Even inference takes place automatically. The knowledge may not be useful or helpful to you, but it happens all the same. The required conditions must be there, that is the only prerequisite.

When the knowledge is of a different nature, it requires preparedness, eligibility. For instance, at school, if you are qualified, prepared, you can understand the subject. Sometimes, you may be ready, but the teacher is not. If the teacher is prepared, and the student is qualified, eligible, eager to know, knowledge will definitely take place. The student must be eligible. Merely because the father is a great mathematician and the mother a physicist and they try to teach their two-year-old child, the child is not going to respond. It is too young; it is not eligible, not ready for knowledge. It can also be that the child is intellectually not very bright or has a learning disability. Naturally, such a child, no matter what its age or genetic lineage, is not going to absorb calculus or particle physics. The *adhikāra*, eligibility to know is not there. You can learn only when you already have some basic knowledge of a given subject for you to build upon. This is how human knowledge has been gathered over the centuries. *Adhikṛtasya adhikārah*, the eligibility is for the already eligible, for one who has accomplished something from where he or she can know more.

ELIGIBILITY FOR SELF-KNOWLEDGE

When it comes to self-knowledge, what is the *adhikāra*, eligibility? It means the teacher, the subject matter, and the student being available, knowledge should take place.

But there is a clause, a condition required here. In Indian logic this condition is called *upādhi* which means, 'if you are ready.' The condition is introduced to account for the realities. The reality is, in spite of my exposure to the teaching, knowledge does not take place. The subject matter here is *ātman*. The teacher and the student are available. If knowledge does not take place, the reason is lack of *adhikāritva*, eligibility or preparedness. In Sanskrit, the eligible person is called *adhikārin*, and the abstract noun of this term is *adhikāritva*, the eligible status. It is this person who is being discussed.

The subject matter is unlike others. If you have covered enough areas in mathematics, you can understand and appreciate calculus. Vedanta is different. You have to be an *adhikārin*. You have to grow into a person who is eligible for this knowledge. Although academic qualifications do help you with the necessary intellectual infrastructure to think logically, clearly and see through false statements, it is not *adhikāritva*. Once a famous person remarked that in the world there is no language greater than Tamil. When I asked him how many languages he knew, his reply was, he was content with just Tamil. His claim that Tamil is the greatest language is obviously false because he does not know the greatness of Tamil language compared to other languages. You need the intellectual capacity to see through the false statement. How can he say Tamil is the greatest language when he does not know other languages? He needs to know not just other languages but also linguistics before comparing languages. Language is a means of communication, a tool, but to dedicate your life to a means of communication when you have nothing to communicate is ridiculous. This is what I call as wrong thinking. Often people do not think properly. You need to think clearly before making categorical statements. Education helps you to think clearly, but it does not make you eligible to know yourself. You may not be academically qualified, but you may be able to gain self-knowledge. For self-knowledge, all you need is a capacity to think cogently.

Beyond eligibility, the question of the individual arises. Who is the person who wants to know? The person is very important because the knowledge, the subject matter is what one wants to be. Generally, in other disciplines of knowledge, you do not want to be the subject matter. For example, when you choose microbiology, you do not want to become a microbe. When you choose geology, you do not want to become a stone or any other mineral. What you want to study, you do not wish to become. You learn the subject as a distinct entity separate from you. In this respect, Vedanta is entirely different.

The subject matter of Vedanta is the fullness, the wholeness that is your nature. It is what you want to be. You will not and cannot settle for anything less. You are like a river rushing towards its source, the ocean. The river will not brook any obstacle. It will struggle to find a way across. Be it mountains, valleys, boulders, it will overcome all of them in its yearning to merge with the ocean. As it nears the ocean, for a few miles upstream, the water is already saline. You cannot distinguish where the river ends and the ocean begins. The ocean appears to welcome the river in its arms. At the sight of its source, the river relaxes. The story of the river is the story of every human soul, its yearning to be free from a sense of limitation, the yearning for fullness.

Everyone loves sleep only because of this yearning for fullness. As we analyse our love for sleep, we come to understand the nature and content of our seeking. It is a fact that everyone loves sleep. Nobody complains that they have to sleep every day, day after day. Nobody has this problem. On the contrary, the love for sleep is so much that everyone first wakes up and gets up later. Perhaps, that is the reason why we wish each other good morning. It is not a good morning at all, since we have to wake up from sleep! Between waking up and getting up, there is a conflict, should I get up or not? It only reveals our intense love for sleep. The reason is, in sleep we experience a freedom from a sense of limitation. This freedom is what we call *mokṣa*, freedom from what we do not want to be.

INNER GROWTH IS BASED ON YOUR INITIATIVE

Returning to Vedanta, the subject is what you want to be, that is freedom from a sense of lack. Naturally, a person has to grow in maturity before he or she becomes eligible for this knowledge. This growth is not natural; it is not physical or biological growth. You can live to be a ninety year old and not be mature. You will age but not grow. The inner person remains a child, a child that cannot face disappointments in life. From losing a balloon to losses in the stock market, you cannot handle the downside of life. You have to grow, which means you need to make the effort. If it is simple biological growth, you need not do anything; nature will take care of it. But inner growth requires initiative and effort on your part. It does not happen naturally.

You do not learn anything without effort on your part. Experience does not teach unless you actively learn from it. People often say that experience teaches. I wish it did. People are what they are, not for want of experiences. There is enough and more experience in everyone's life. You need not experience everything personally to learn. You can learn from other's experience too. If you have to learn only from your own experience, human civilisation would not be where it is today. If you have to know what electrocution is through experience, would you be alive to share the knowledge? Therefore, it is not for want of experience that you do not know; it is because you do not learn from it. Learning comes with initiative. When you make use of an opportunity to learn, it is an initiative. A good example is your choosing to come here to listen to my lecture. You have come here through your initiative. Further, areas of learning are vast. You may know one area well, and others not as well or not at all. In order to know a particular subject, you have to take the initiative. Discovering love is no different. You need to take the initiative to know, to discover what love is.

If you can command a degree of love, a degree of the meaning of love which is freedom from limitation, from division, then I would say you are mature. The loving will be naturally compassionate, naturally sympathetic, understanding, giving, and yielding. It is the loving person who is truly eligible for discovering that he or she is the content of love, which is fullness. It is this fullness that manifests in the form of love. The dynamic form of *ānanda* is love. Unrelated it is *ānanda*; related it is love. It undergoes various changes as the objects you relate to, differ.

How to discover love for yourself

You must understand that you need to have an infrastructure to receive love. If you cannot receive love, you cannot give either. You cannot command love. You can be a loving person only when you love yourself. If you do not, you cannot receive love. You cannot even take love. Since you do not have love for yourself, if another seems to have love for you, that person becomes an object of obsession. You will strangulate the very thing you love. You will destroy that love because it becomes a need. It is no longer something that you can absorb. Even if someone says, "I love you," you will question because you do not have love for yourself. If you can discover love for yourself as a person, as an individual, you have an infrastructure to absorb love. Then you can give love without loss, without reservation. As we saw earlier, the self is love. In fact, the self is everything. It is the content of love itself.

Everything is given

Having said that, is it possible to love the self? If you look at yourself as an individual, you find that it is difficult, if not impossible, to have self-love. Your body, mind, family, situation and so on, all of these have been given to you.

The reasons could be on the basis of either genetics or *karma*. If you take one more step from genetics, it becomes *karma*. Whatever be the reason, the fact is, you have been placed in a particular situation over which you have no choice. Your parentage, physical body, mind, senses, emotions, intellect, memory, all these are given to you. The world, the sun, the solar system, the black holes and the galaxies are also given. The basic forces, the laws within the whole structure in this expanding universe are given. Everything is given to you. Everything, known, not yet known, that which cannot be known at all, all these constitute the world, the *jagat*. It is a given reality. Everything has its place in the scheme of things. The scientists try to find out their places, their roles. They are given the wherewithal to explore the phenomena around them. Matter or energy is neither created nor destroyed; it is only in one form or another. This is how the *jagat* is. Everything is given.

You can also look at the world from a different perspective, the perspective of orders. There is physical order, biological order, psychological order and so on. These orders constitute the universe which is given to you. This universal order is what we call *niyati, bhautika-niyati*, physical order, and much more. Everything is a system, an order. When you study animals for example, you find an interconnected world wherein the organisms manifest a similarity. It is the reason why we experiment with rats and monkeys in medical research. If a particular medication works on either of these animals, the scientists feel confident that they can try it on human beings. It is because of the order, the physiological order.

Another order is the psychological order. A neglect or lack of understanding of this order has contributed to the many problems you face in the family and in society today. Your parents did not know nor did their parents before them. Earlier it was a highly structured society without too many choices. Each person knew fairly well what his or her future would be. Professions and careers were passed on from father to son. There were no surprises or anxieties because competition was minimal. Without competition, there was inner leisure which contributed to the growth of the classical arts.

Today, society presents a completely different picture. Children are pushed into schools before they can even walk. They have to compete when they are least equipped to do so. The child feels abandoned and this creates tremendous stress within the child. Unable to bear the mental pain, the child pushes the pain inside. The unconscious is nothing but the pain gathered in the first four or five years of a child's life. Moreover, it takes years and years of processing to resolve the unconscious, if one cares to process it at all. Without processing it, the problem that one is not loved or cared for will continue even if one lives to be ninety.

A child is incapable of handling pain. When it is sent to school at the tender age of two or three, it feels that its Gods, its parents, have abandoned it. The child feels that it is in some way responsible for being sent away. It cannot afford to displease its Gods, the almighty mother and father. So, the child pretends to love school and smiles at its parents. Deep within, it blames itself because mother cannot be wrong. At a tender age the child concludes, it is being sent to school because it is not good enough for its parents. From then on, the feeling of 'not being good enough' builds up with each hurt and pain. Later, it comes out as, "My son does not love me. He does not write at all. My children have abandoned me." This is an eighty-year-old father's feeling. It is the same as the conclusion of a three-year-old child. It continues throughout your life if you do not pay attention to yourself. This is the psychological order.

Besides these orders, you have the cognitive order which is also known as the epistemological order. It deals with how you gather knowledge and whether the knowledge is right or wrong. Fundamentally, you are a cognitive person. You can manage your life only cognitively. It cannot be otherwise. The emotional person cannot manage life. If the emotions are not understood, they will take the cognitive person for a ride. There is another order, that of the memory, which helps you to record and erase many of your experiences. It is amazing that you remember something only for a few minutes or a few days and then it gets erased. Selective destruction helps to make space for important facts to be stored. There are various types of memory such as short-term memory, long-term, semantic, episodic, conscious and unconscious. There is an order in memory, which means that there is a law operating in this field. Memory is included in the epistemological order. This in turn lies within the psychological order, an order within an order.

It is important to understand that all the different orders form one order that is Brahmāṇḍa. It is one huge order. The question is from whom does this order come? Who is the giver?

Is there a distance between the giver and the given? As you inquire into the order, you find it is intelligent, since lot of knowledge is involved in each one. Further, where there is knowledge, a conscious being is definitely involved. If you look at any part of your body, you find each one is intelligently put together. Be it your eyes, ears, heart, liver and others, they reveal knowledge, tremendous knowledge. It is true of the entire *jagat*. If the given is so intelligently put together, it must presuppose a giver with the necessary knowledge. Who is this giver?

This is the beauty of the Veda whose vision alone we can accept and assimilate. The giver is neither far away in heaven nor is heaven separate from the giver. The entire *jagat* is non-separate from the giver since the material necessary for creation rests with the said giver. The maker and the material cannot be separate; they are non-separate. If they are separate, there must be something that separates. If the separating factor is space, space itself is part of the creation, just as time is. Therefore, the maker and the material being one and the same, the entire *jagat* is the manifestation of Īśvara. Words like omniscience and its meaning cannot be understood, unless you are omniscient yourself. The only way you can understand Īśvara is by knowing he is in the form of this intelligent order, an order that is complete. The whole order includes everything that is yet to be discovered or that which may not be discovered at all. Consequently, you appreciate Īśvara in the form of the various orders such as physical, biological, psychological and so on.

The entire order is Īśvara, *sat-cit-ānanda* with the power of *māyā*, the *śakti*. An appreciation of this order is not a belief; it requires understanding. It is purely cognitive. It means that an awareness of what you call God, Īśvara, gives you space. When I say space, it means an inner space within the psychological order, to observe your thoughts, your reactions, including your love or dislike for yourself. A good analogy would be a machine with a motor, revolving some revolutions per minute. The motor is not aware of its revolutions. However, suppose it is aware that it revolves at some hundred or thousand revolutions per minute, the motor is no longer mechanical. It is an insight. Similarly, the moment you become aware that there is nothing wrong with you or with anybody, you are no longer mechanical.

The fact is that there is nothing wrong with anybody in this world. There are no criminals; there are only crimes and there are people given to crimes. It is caused by anger against the society, the establishment. Some of the people in jails suffer from MPD, multiple personality disorders. You may wonder why the person commits the same crime in the same manner again and again, only to get caught by the police. There is no doubt that these jailbirds are not criminals. They are not even given to crime; they suffer from multiple personality disorder. They themselves do not know what is going on. They require proper counselling. Therefore, I say that there are no criminals; there are people given to crimes.

TALK 6

APPRECIATING ĪŚVARA AS PSYCHOLOGICAL
AND DHARMIC ORDER

If you understand you are within the order, that nothing happens in your mind outside the order, it means you are in order. When someone says, "I love you," it means he or she accepts you as you are, without reservations. It is within the order, the order that is Īśvara. Īśvara cannot be surprised by anybody simply because he is the order. He is the all-knowledge order. In the awareness, the understanding of that order, you can completely relax. The result is love, nothing but love; love for yourself and for others. There is no other way of finding self-love. Without Īśvara, you cannot discover love for yourself. It is impossible to love anybody or anything without discovering self-love. Everything in this world you can love only if you have love for yourself. This love manifests as sympathy, compassion and so on.

INNER SPACE HELPS YOU
UNDERSTAND YOUR EMOTIONS

What you basically seek happens to be yourself. The love for *sādhya*, what is to be accomplished, an end that you love, is already *siddha*, accomplished. The problem is that despite an exposure to the teaching, it is difficult to accept this fact. Even if you are able to see this fact, you are unable to reap the benefit of the knowledge. In other words, you are not loving or compassionate, spontaneously.

You are happy when you see yourself a loving person. If you are not happy, you can neither love nor be loving. Since you do not often come across such loving persons, you look upon a very loving person as a saint. That person becomes special, a holy person. The fact is, everyone has the potential to be a saint. Saintliness is your nature. It is characterised by love, compassion, understanding, sympathy, giving, a readiness to help and much more.

In day-to-day life, however, the opposite seems to be the norm. People are more prone to hatred, jealousy, dislike and so on. These opposing traits inhibit the natural ones. Consequently, you do not need to cultivate love; you have to neutralise the inhibiting factors. Therefore, our *śāstra* completely differs from theologies and religious preaching.

The first inhibiting factor is ignorance; it is not easy to remove. Inspite of an opportunity to study the *śāstra*, exposure to the teaching for a length of time, you do not see or understand what the nature of the self is. There seems to be some *pratibandhaka*s, obstructing factors, which are due to emotional problems. They hold the cognitive person hostage. The emotional person appears to have the power to decide how loving or how happy you can be. It is very important, therefore, to understand the emotional person. In order to understand your emotions, you need some inner space, for which you need a cognitive change. You need to learn to relax in the awareness, in the understanding of your emotions.

By relaxation I do not refer to the many techniques that are offered in the 'spiritual' market today. Every newspaper carries announcements of various workshops peddling techniques of how to relax, breathe, meditate and so on. I am not talking of such relaxation. Any technique wears out. It is useful only for some time. Later, it becomes mechanical and you grow out of it. You start looking out for newer and newer techniques. It becomes an endless, futile search.

RELAXING IN THE PSYCHOLOGICAL ORDER THAT IS ĪŚVARA

The relaxation I am talking of is born of understanding the reality of the world. I had said earlier that things are given and they are not separate from the giver. The giver is Īśvara who is in the form of one total order consisting of many orders. We have seen the various orders such as physical, biological, psychological and so on. The cognitive order, including memory, lies within this psychological order.

Cognition and memory help you recall and recognise persons, objects and situations. Even emotions are included in this order. Anger, for instance, is memory based. It comes from the unconscious, the unconscious memory. It is the cognitive order that also helps you appreciate Īśvara as one vast order that is the creation. It is equally responsible for the feeling of low self-esteem and self-loathe.

When you compare yourself with the vastness of the world, one obvious consequence will be a sense of 'I am not good enough.' It is due to lack of self-worth. Each one of us has a niggling self-doubt, 'Am I all right? Am I acceptable? Am I normal?' The doubt persists mainly because situations get the better of you. The word normal means being consistent in your responses. However, you find that your responses are unpredictable. Mornings you smile, by evening you are cantankerous. Why do the moods and responses change? It means you have no control over your moods, your emotional responses. They control your actions because they stem from the unconscious over which you have no control.

The unconscious repeatedly tells you, 'you are no good, you are not acceptable,' and so on. The various situations that you face further confirm your self-non-acceptance. This is within the psychological order. Psychology has a limited scope even though it helps you to understand yourself in a broad manner. It restates your emotional condition for clarity, but it does not resolve your emotional problems.

You can now understand that emotional life of a person has its roots in the unconscious, the *kaṣāya*. However, you need to recognise it is also Īśvara. It is very important. You have to leave psychology aside and move on to realities. From a psychological reality you turn to cognitive reality. Cognitive reality is to understand this is order, the psychological order, and the order is Īśvara.

Living in harmony with the
dharmic order that is Īśvara

I include one more order, the law, the order of *dharma*, which is also Īśvara. The reason is, there is right and wrong in the world. While good and bad are judgements, emotional responses, right and wrong are realities. For instance, if you wish to open a door or turn a key, there is a right way of doing it and a wrong way. Even in speech, there is a right way and a wrong way of pronouncing words. Right and wrong are not opinions; they are not personal notions. It is just that things are either right or wrong. There is right and wrong means of achieving an end. What is important is the means must be in keeping with the end, for it is the end that decide the means. Right and wrong have always been there but good and bad are your judgements; they are relative. What is good for you may be bad for another. There is no bad person, only people given to wrong actions. If you continue to analyse you will find you are much more alive to the realities of the world. If not, you will be living in your own judgemental world, a world of your projection.

Right and wrong are what we call in Sanskrit as *dharma* and *adharma*. They are not rules given by few wise men, demanding implicit obedience from you. If right and wrong have to be taught, then they cannot be called universal. Universality means everyone commonly senses, which is why the term common sense. For instance, if you ask anyone, an Eskimo, a Harvard professor, a Boston Brahmin, a Chinese peasant, or any other, "Do you want to be cheated? Do you want to be hurt? Do you want to be robbed? Do you want to be taken advantage of?" Uniformly, every one of them will reply in the negative. No one wants to be hurt, robbed, cheated, or taken advantage of. Every one knows that the other expects the same from him or her. It is commonly sensed knowledge or common sense. Knowledge, in turn, implies a reality. There is no knowledge without an object. If there is no object, you cannot call it knowledge. The criminal laws, civil laws, are based upon this commonly sensed law, called *sāmānya-dharma*. Just as a baby monkey senses that if it falls down it will get hurt, and therefore clings on to its mother for safety, these commonly sensed rules or laws form the basis of *sāmānya-dharma*. The monkey senses it instinctively; it is a survivor. Every living organism has this survival instinct embedded in its software. It is programmed to sense danger, to know how to survive. It is amazing how, without being taught, a baby monkey knows so much.

In a human being, the common sense is manifest within a matrix of norms to make the necessary choices. You can sense these norms without being taught. Therefore, these norms, *dharma*, exist in your head and not somewhere outside, in books or rules given by a few people. *Dharma* is something that is inborn; if not there would be a lacuna in the creation, which is neither acceptable nor true. It is not as though a human being has been given the faculty of choice but God forgot to give the norms to exercise the choice. It would mean that every one is out to destroy the other, a grave error on the part of God, the creator. It would be the mother of all manufacturing errors.

We do not say God appeared at a given point in time and laid down the rules of *dharma* and *adharma*. The argument that the laws of *dharma* were laid down at a given time in history is based on the concept of God in heaven, who is separate from the creation. You have seen that the creator, the giver, can never be separate from the creation, the given. Everything that is here is Īśvara. It means every law is a manifestation of Īśvara. Every form is the lord's form. *Dharma* is not different; it is the very manifestation of Īśvara.

We do not say God gave us a mandate. We say the mandate itself is God. It is ridiculous to say that you believe in God. It is not a question of belief; it is a matter to be understood. If you do not care about Vedanta but live a life of *dharma*, you have *ānanda* because you are in conformity with Īśvara, but without knowing it. If you choose to know, the knowledge makes the difference between success and failure. It makes you understand that what is, is Īśvara.

When you look at *dharma* and *adharma* as another order, you find, where there is *dharma* there is also *karma*. Our *śāstras* do not introduce *dharma* and *adharma*, they confirm what you already sense and add another element, that of *karma*. It tells you that you may escape all the man-made laws but you cannot escape the laws of Īśvara. The law of *karma* will catch up with you either in this life or in the hereafter. You have to experience the result of your action. If yours was a reaching out action, prayer or service, the result is *puṇya*, positive results. It is credited to your account; while the opposite actions produce what we call *pāpa*, negative results. Both *puṇya* and *pāpa* are *adṛṣṭa*, unseen. *Puṇya* translates into pleasant situations, *sukha*, while *pāpa* brings unpleasant experiences, *duḥkha*. This is law of *karma*.

Without the law of *dharma*, there is no *karma*. Any living being that does not have the faculty of choice is called *vimukta*. It means, they are free from *dharma* and *adharma* and consequently from *puṇya* and *pāpa*. If a tiger kills a goat or a donkey kicks, they do not attract *pāpa*, since their actions are instinctive and not born of deliberate freewill. However, if you or I should eat an animal, it is definitely *pāpa* because we can choose. Food is basically vegetarian; only a prepared meal is non-vegetarian. If you deliberately exercise your choice to eat by causing harm to another living being, it is definitely *adharma* and the result is *pāpa*.

Our *śāstra* intervenes only to the extent of pointing out the results of *dharmic* and *adharmic* actions that is *puṇya* and *pāpa*. It is a belief no doubt, but a belief that has some logic and can be assimilated, since it does not conradict your experiences in the world. A wrong action on your part results in some punishment, a prison sentence, a psychological punishment such as guilt, fear and so on.

Our *śāstra* adds one more to the list, and that is karmic punishment. The law of *karma* does not take into account the punishment meted out here in this world. It follows its own rules and methods. One part of the law is *dharma* and the other is *karma*. It is another manifestation of Īśvara. By following *dharma*, you are not obliging Īśvara, but you are in harmony with Īśvara. In life, things are not always black or white; it is often in shades of grey. At such times, you need help to choose what is appropriate action and what is not.

Words such as appropriate or inappropriate are variable depending on time, culture, society and so on. Table manners, social etiquette, customs and other patterns of behaviour require some training. What is accepted in one country may not be in another. In the West, it is considered polite to talk during a meal, while in India it is not. In India eating with your hands is the norm while in the West it is not.

When you are in doubt, the best thing to do is to seek help. It is the intelligent way to live. Ask a person who is supposed to know the nuances of *dharma* and *karma*.

The *śāstra* also warns you to be careful regarding the person from whom you seek help. They should not benefit from your actions. They should be *alūkṣāḥ dharmakāmāḥ*, dispassionate, who will not take advantage of a situation. It is not wrong to be ignorant, but it is foolish to continue to be so.

Thus, the order of *dharma* and *karma* is part of one vast order that is Īśvara. When you look upon your psycholgical and emotional issues, you understand, there is a reason for their existence. It means you are within the order. It is very important to understand this. You need not blame yourself for lack of self-love, or for your sense of persecution. There are many others like you and they are all within the order. It is due to some psychological background and you can resolve them with help. The background is part of Īśvara's law. This understanding helps you validate your feelings. It also helps to prevent you from victimising others. The more you validate your feelings, the freer you become. It is the greatest truth in managing your emotions, in living. The more you are aware of Īśvara, more you appreciate life. In your appreciation of Īśvara, you find the greatest therapist, a super therapist who is always with you.

ACCEPTING MYSELF AS BEING IN ORDER
IS GATEWAY TO RELAXATION

The moment you accept yourself as being in order, as being a part of the vast order that is Īśvara, your life becomes successful. When you say, you are fine, you are all right, it is different from saying, you think you are fine, you think you are all right. The thinking becomes another superimposition which is not at all helpful. At first, you felt you were no good. Later, with some positive thinking, you superimpose a feeling of being fine. One superimposition is bad enough. To have a double superimposition is impossible. It is just a cosmetic cover from the many workshops on positive thinking, relaxation and so on. The positive effect lasts for barely one day and the old feeling of 'I am not good enough' or 'I am not acceptable' returns with bag and baggage. Therefore, it is very important to be aware of and appreciate the presence of Īśvara as the order that pervades you. He pervades you in all your emotions, your cognitive skills. In everything there is the presence of Īśvara. It is an expression of the law, the order that is Īśvara.

If you understand this, then the behaviour of the person or persons you are related to, is because of the order. The order includes the capacity to change. You can work towards the change. It may require more effort on your part and more time to bring about a change. You need to understand this clearly. You cannot say, 'Īśvara is all pervasive except in my mother-in-law.' You cannot allow your emotions to interfere. She may have her own problems and so has her daughter- in-law. Everyone is an angel if only each one understands Īśvara as the order that is. When you relax in your awareness of Īśvara, you can take people as they are, with compassion and understanding. You become pragmatic.

Once I was asked, "Swamiji, if I become loving, do you think that I will be the same when I deal with a snake? Will I accept the snake is also Īśvara? Will it stop biting me?"

Yes, it is true that the snake is also Īśvara. However, you need some pragmatism here. You must remember that pragmatism and wisdom are also Īśvara. It is your nature to turn away from danger, and it is the nature of the snake to bite you. Both these natural traits are Īśvara. I must understand things in their proper perspective.

LOVE IS FREE OF CONTROL

It is your own anxieties, fears, your agenda for others that separates you from the world, from understanding. You cannot enjoy your family, much less your children. You are unable to share their childhood, their growing years, the friendship of their adulthood. Your anxiety for their future, providing for their security, prevent you from reaching out to them freely, whole heartedly. The problem does not lie in planning for the future. Every prudent person will definitely plan. The problem is, you want them to obey you implicitly. You do not think that your child is an independent person. You think that your child is an extension of you. This is where the problem lies.

If you understand a child is born of you, yes, but it is not a part of you. It is like a candle lit from another candle; it is not half a candle. Similarly, from life is born another life. The child has its own body, mind, senses, *ātman*; it is complete, *pūrṇa*. It is whole from a whole, *pūrṇāt pūrṇam*. Please understand that it is a growing whole. It is a beautiful thought. The child is given to you. Born of you; you are a *nimitta*, cause. It is the same Īśvara's order and you are merely an instrument.

Lack of understanding denies you to enjoy your children. It is not because you cannot love. Which parent does not love or care? The problem is, you consider the child as part of you. What you think is good for the child, the child must also think so. Often when I visit people's homes, the parents want their child to chant or sing for the Swami. "Come, chant *śuklāmbaradharam*. Come on." The child protests. It is asserting its independence. The parents cannot understand and are disappointed. They have not understood that the child is not a part of them. Please understand this well. A child is independent; it is whole. Learn to enjoy the whole. You can never enjoy a part, but you can enjoy the whole. The love for your child is inhibited by your agenda because for you love means control. When you say, "I love you," it means the person whom you love must obey you. You cannot trust simply because you have no self-love. If you can learn to relax, you will understand that love is not control. Do you know why you control? It is part of the psychological order. You control because you could not trust your parents. You could not communicate with your parents. Perhaps, it was a problem caused by alcohol. Whatever be the reason, between the parents and you, the child, there was neither communication nor understanding.

As a child, you had to figure out how to win your parents' approval, your Gods' approval. Hence, you had to ensure that you were right all the time. You had to draw lines within which alone there was predictability; there was no vulnerability. Outside the lines, you were vulnerable. You had no control and it became a problem. You tried to manipulate situations as well as you could, but things always got out of your control. Therefore, you need to be aware that you tend to control. You can say it out aloud, "I tend to control, and I think control is love." It can help you understand it is control, it is not love, although behind the control there is love. That is why there is so much pain, the pain of a child that was not understood.

It is important to understand that control is not love; possessiveness is not love; ownership is not love. Often, you think that anything you love, you should have, should own. You love this flower and at once you reach out and pluck it. No, it is not necessary. Let it be where it is. Let the stars be where they are; you love them as they are. Another point I wish to make is you need not marry whomever you love. It is an important thing to know. You love the person you are married to. You need not marry every person you love. You just love, nothing more. It does not have any other connotation. It is simple.

DISCOVER LOVE BY LOVING

The truth is, you are love; you may or may not know. When you give or receive love, you are the same person. When you to extend your love to another, it does not matter even if you do not have love. You fake it and make it. When you reach out and extend love, the very action brings out the loving person in you. Love becomes real because love is you. All you require is to know and understand the fact.

As you look further into yourself, you see the presence of Īśvara in the form of your emotions. You accept them as valid.

You also accept that they have a background. It makes you normal in every way. You must understand this well. Every one of you should say, "I am normal." When you say, "I am normal," you will find there is nothing inhibiting your love.

What is love? It is nothing but compassion which is sympathy and which in turn is understanding. The more loving you are, the easier it is for you to understand what the *śāstra* says. It says, *ātman*, the self is whole. The wholeness naturally comes to manifest; it does not remain as an ideal. It is this wholeness that you love. When all that is here is one whole, where is the question of your not loving? When you understand this, you have discovered love. There is nothing here but love.

Oṁ tat sat

For a list of our other publications,
please visit the website at:
www.avrpt.com

...or contact :

ARSHA VIDYA RESEARCH
AND PUBLICATION TRUST
32 / 4 Sir Desika Road,
Mylapore Chennai 600 004
Telefax : 044 - 2499 7131
Email   : avrandpt@gmail.com
Website : www.avrpt.com

ARSHA VIDYA GURUKULAM
Anaikatti P.O.
Coimbatore 641 108
Ph   : 0422 - 2657001
Fax   : 0422 - 2657002
Email   : office@arshavidya.in
Website : www.arshavidya.in

SWAMI DAYANANDA ASHRAM
Purani Jhadi, P.B.No. 30
Rishikesh, Uttaranchal 249 201
Telefax : 0135 - 2430769
Email   : ashrambookstore@yahoo.com
Website : www.dayananda.org

ARSHA VIDYA GURUKULAM
P.O. Box 1059. Pennsylvania
PA 18353, USA
Ph   : 001 - 570 - 992 - 2339
Email   : avp@epix.net
Website : www.arshavidya.org

Our publications are also available at all leading bookstores and
downloadable through the 'Teachings of Swami Dayananda'
APP for Android and Apple devices.